MY ROWS AND PILES OF COINS

BY TOLOLWA M. MOLLEL

ILLUSTRATED BY E. B. LEWIS

This edition is published by special arrangement with Clarion Books, a Houghton Mifflin Company imprint.

Grateful acknowledgment is made to Clarion Books, a Houghton Mifflin Company imprint for permission to reprint *My Rows and Piles of Coins* by Tololwa M. Mollel, illustrated by E. B. Lewis. Text copyright © 1999 by Tololwa M. Mollel; illustrations copyright © 1999 by E. B. Lewis.

Printed in China

ISBN 10 0-15-365118-0
ISBN 13 978-0-15-365118-2

2 3 4 5 6 7 8 9 10   895   17 16 14 13 12 11 10 09 08

In memory of my grandfather and *murete*, Lotasarwaki Marti
–T.M.M.

In loving memory of Dorothy Briley
–E.B.L.

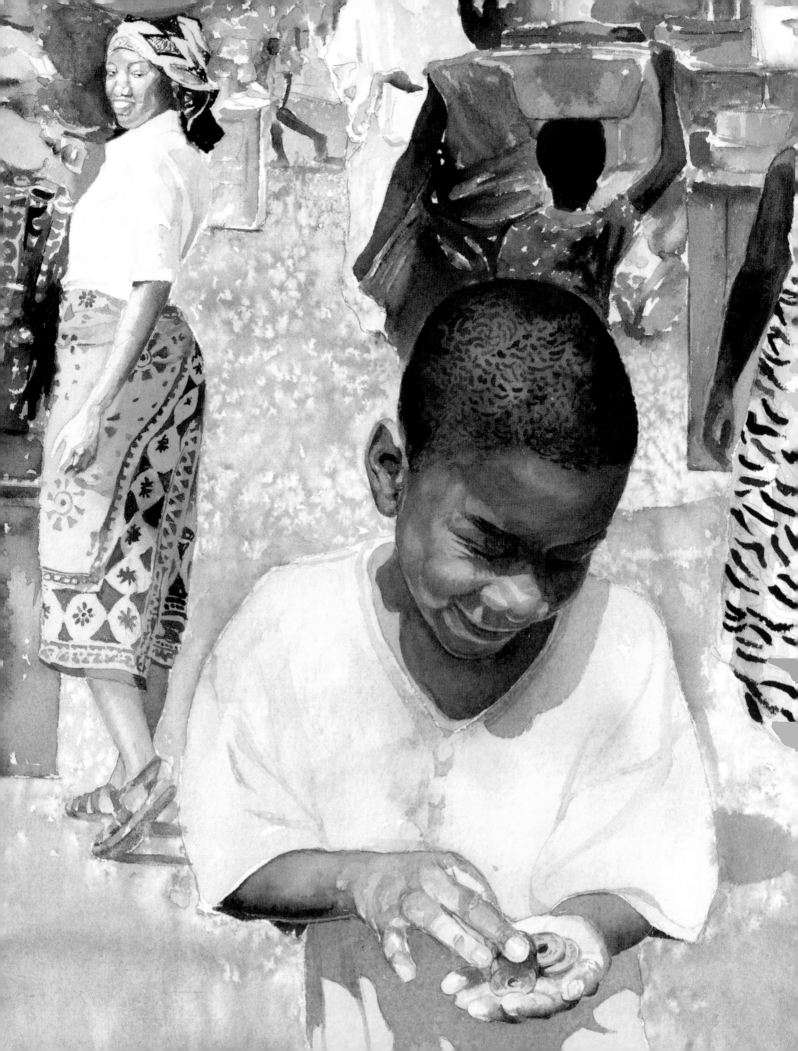

After a good day at the market, my mother, Yeyo, gave me five whole ten-cent coins. I gaped at the money until Yeyo nudged me. "Saruni, what are you waiting for? Go and buy yourself something."

I plunged into the market. I saw roasted peanuts, *chapati*, rice cakes, and *sambusa*. There were wooden toy trucks, kites, slingshots, and marbles. My heart beat excitedly. I wanted to buy everything, but I clutched my coins tightly in my pocket.

At the edge of the market, I stopped. In a neat sparkling row stood several big new bicycles. One of them was decorated all over with red and blue.

That's what I would buy!

For some time now, Murete, my father, had been teaching me to ride his big, heavy bicycle. If only I had a bicycle of my own!

A gruff voice startled me. "What are you looking for, little boy?"

I turned and bumped into a tall skinny man, who laughed at my confusion. Embarrassed, I hurried back to Yeyo.

That night, I dropped five ten-cent coins into my secret money box. It held other ten-cent coins Yeyo had given me for helping with market work on Saturdays. By the dim light of a lantern, I feasted my eyes on the money. I couldn't believe it was all mine.

I emptied the box,
arranged all the coins in piles
and the piles in rows.
Then I counted the coins
and thought about the bicycle
I longed to buy.

Every day after school, when I wasn't helping Yeyo to prepare supper, I asked Murete if I could ride his bicycle. He held the bicycle steady while I rode around, my toes barely touching the pedals.

Whenever Murete let go, I wobbled, fell off, or crashed into things and among coffee trees. Other children from the neighborhood had a good laugh watching me.

Go on, laugh, I thought, sore but determined. Soon I would be like a cheetah on wheels, racing on errands with my very own bicycle!

Saturday after Saturday, we took goods to market, piled high on Yeyo's head and on my squeaky old wooden wheelbarrow. We sold dried beans and maize, pumpkins, spinach, bananas, firewood, and eggs.

My money box grew heavier.

I emptied the box,
arranged the coins in piles
and the piles in rows.
Then I counted the coins
and thought about
the blue and red bicycle.

After several more lessons Murete let me ride on my own while he shouted instructions. *"Eyes up, arms straight, keep pedaling, slow down!"* I enjoyed the breeze on my face, the pedals turning smoothly under my feet, and, most of all, Yeyo's proud smile as she watched me ride. How surprised she would be to see my new bicycle! And how grateful she would be when I used it to help her on market days!

The heavy March rains came. The ground became so muddy, nobody went to market. Instead, I helped Yeyo with house chores. When it wasn't raining, I helped Murete on the coffee farm. We pruned the coffee trees and put fallen leaves and twigs around the coffee stems. Whenever I could, I practiced riding Murete's bicycle.

It stopped raining in June. Not long after, school closed. Our harvest—fresh maize and peas, sweet potatoes, vegetables, and fruits—was so big, we went to market on Saturdays *and* Wednesdays. My money box grew heavier and heavier.

I emptied the box,
arranged the coins in piles
and the piles in rows.
Then I counted the coins
and thought about the bicycle
I would buy.

A few days later I grew confident enough to try to ride a loaded bicycle. With Murete's help, I strapped a giant pumpkin on the carrier behind me. When I attempted to pedal, the bicycle wobbled so dangerously that Murete, alongside me, had to grab it.

"All right, Saruni, the load is too heavy for you," he said, and I got off. Mounting the bicycle to ride back to the house, he sighed wearily. "And hard on my bones, which are getting too old for pedaling."

I practiced daily with smaller loads, and slowly I learned to ride a loaded bicycle. No more pushing the squeaky old wheelbarrow, I thought. I would ride with my load tall and proud on my bicycle—just like Murete!

On the first Saturday after school opened in July, we went to market as usual. Late in the afternoon, after selling all we had, Yeyo sat talking with another trader.

I set off into the crowd. I wore an old coat Murete had handed down to me for chilly July days like today. My precious coins were wrapped in various bundles inside the oversize pockets of the coat.

I must be the richest boy in the world, I thought, feeling like a king. *I can buy anything.*

The tall skinny man was polishing his bicycles as I came up. "I want to buy a bicycle," I said, and brought out my bundles of coins.

The man whistled in wonder as I unwrapped the money carefully on his table. "How many coins have you got there?"

Proudly, I told him. "Three hundred and five."

"Three hundred and . . . five," he muttered. "Mmh, that's . . . thirty shillings and fifty cents." He exploded with laughter. "A whole bicycle . . . for thirty shillings . . . and fifty cents?"

His laugh followed me as I walked away with my bundles of coins, deeply disappointed.

On our way home, Yeyo asked what was wrong.

I had to tell her everything.

"You saved all your money for a bicycle to help me?" she asked. I could tell she was amazed and touched. "How nice of you!" As for the tall skinny man, she scoffed, "*Oi!* What does he know? Of course you will buy a bicycle. One day you will."

Her kind words did not cheer me.

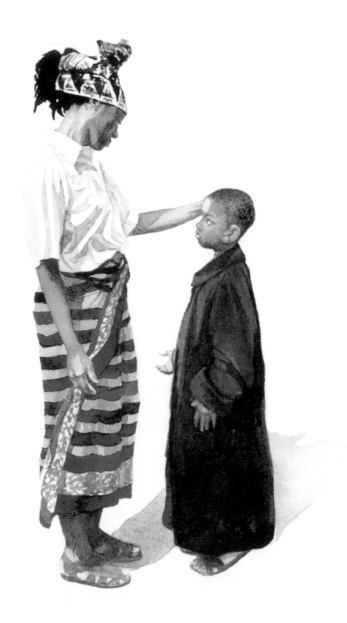

The next afternoon, the sound of a *pikipiki* filled the air, *tuk-tuk-tuk-tuk-tuk*. I came out of the house and stared in astonishment. Murete was perched on an orange motorbike.

He cut the engine and dismounted. Then, chuckling at my excited questions about the *pikipiki*, he headed into the house.

When Murete came out, Yeyo was with him, and he was wheeling his bicycle. "I want to sell this to you. For thirty shillings and fifty cents." He winked at me.

Surprised, I stared at Murete. How did he know about my secret money box? I hadn't told him anything.

Then, suddenly, I realized the wonderful thing that had just happened. "My bicycle, I have my very own bicycle!" I said, and it didn't matter at all that it wasn't decorated with red and blue. Within moments, I had brought Murete my money box.

Murete gave Yeyo the box. Yeyo, in turn, gave it to me. Puzzled, I looked from Yeyo to Murete and to Yeyo again.

"You're giving it . . . back to me?"

Yeyo smiled. "It's a reward for all your help to us."

"Thank you, thank you!" I cried gleefully.

The next Saturday, my load sat tall and proud on my bicycle, which I walked importantly to market. I wasn't riding it because Yeyo could never have kept up.

Looking over at Yeyo, I wished she didn't have to carry such a big load on her head.

If only I had a cart to pull behind my bicycle, I thought, *I could lighten her load!*

That night I emptied the box,
arranged all the coins in piles
and the piles in rows.
Then I counted the coins
and thought about the cart
I would buy. . . .

AUTHOR'S NOTE

The money in the story is Tanzanian currency of the early 1960s (the time of the story and of my childhood in Northern Tanzania). A ten-cent coin was thick and red, with a hole in the middle, and was a significant bit of money then. Ten ten-cent coins, or one hundred cents, made up one shilling, a silver coin. Eight shillings were roughly equivalent to one dollar. Though bikes didn't cost as much then as they do now, at 150 to 500 shillings they were still too expensive for many Tanzanians to buy for recreation or for their children. A family might own a bicycle to be used for work and for essential transportation. That's still the case in Tanzania today, particularly in rural areas.

chapati (chah PAH tee): fried flat round bread made from layered rolled dough (Swahili)

Murete (moo reh teh): Among the Arusha Maasai every child, before it is born, is designated as a younger "version" of an older family member—a parent, grandparent, uncle, or aunt. The child calls this family member Murete, a term of affection. In the story, Saruni is the younger "version" of his father (Maasai)

Oi! (oy): an exasperated or dismissive expression (Maasai)

pikipiki (picky picky): a motorbike or motorcycle (Swahili)

sambusa (sahm BOO sah): little triangular sealed pouch of dough stuffed with spiced vegetables, meat, or both and deep-fried (Swahili)

Saruni (sah ROO nee): a boy's name (Maasai)

tuk-tuk-tuk-tuk-tuk (took-took-took-took-took): the sound of an engine (Maasai)

Yeyo (yey YOH): mother (Maasai)